Raising Happy Toddlers

THE ULTIMATE GUIDE FOR PARENTS TO RAISING HAPPY AND HELTHY CHILDREN

SHANIA WALKER

TABLE OF CONTENTS

Foreword

"Children are great imitators. So give them something great to imitate." —Anonymous

Children are naturally known to be full of happiness and cheerfulness in life. Their lifestyle is based on what they see and what they believe.

Nevertheless, it is natural that children may occasionally experience fear. Just like adults, children face several difficulties that prevent them from enjoying their childhood to the fullest.

As they grow up, children must learn to deal with different types of fears.

They occasionally come across intimidating circumstances, such as starting a new school, performing in front of a large audience, or dealing with a bully at school.

Unfortunately, many parents show little concern for their kids, even when they express fears. A child might develop panic attacks and depression as a result of this poor parenting style.

This is the absolute last thing you want to avoid happening to them if you love them, so be sure to provide them with the comfort they require whenever their fears arise.

This is why this book has been written. In this book, you will get the necessary information to assist your child in overcoming life's obstacles.

So, start reading and discover all the possibilities you have for the development of your child's life.

Chapter 1:

Helping Kids Overcome Fear Of Going To School

It is a big challenge for the majority of children particularly preschoolers and kindergartens to separate from the atmosphere they're familiar with, their comfort zone, and most especially their parents and guidance should learn how to manage this kind of situation with the following suggestions, you can make the entire process go more smoothly and easily for them.

Ensure Smooth Transition

If your child appears to be terrified to enter school, he or she is most likely worried about being separated from you, it is upon the parent to smooth the transition for the child.

This kind of situation can be easily handled by taking the child to the school for a visit, and repeating it a few times before the new school year begins.

Organizing a tour can stimulate their interest in school, take your child around and point at objects and show him different activities, make them participate in some school events, like competing in a race with other kids, and allow them to utilize the playground.

Your child's confidence will increase when he/she gets familiar with new faces.

When a child goes to his or her new school and walks in with a smile on his or her face and then looks at you with a smile, he is sending you a message that he'll be safe, and he can be happy while being there.

If your child sticks up with you like a fastener during the class session, you must make morning routines consistent, while making goodbyes brief, a long farewell scene can make the child think preschool is bad and this will trigger your child's fear.

Immediately you take your leave, the class teacher would have to get your child distracted by indulging him in any kind of activity he loves.

Give him a note or place a giant heart on his lunch box, and I could be a hug, handshake, followed by a see you later "alligator".

Your main objective is to have your child attend class and return to school daily.

When a proper plan is implemented and changes are achieved, the child becomes confident and enjoys going to school, However, a therapist or psychiatrist may be required if the school fear is severe.

However, a therapist or psychiatrist may be required if this persists.

If you notice that your child is anxious about using the restroom, you should follow up by making an in-depth investigation of the cause.

If your child does not have enough time to get to the bathroom, this may also cause him grief.

Is he afraid because the toilet flushes so quickly? Or is he experiencing panic because one of his classmates crawls beneath the stand door? Make him discuss his anxieties, and thereafter you should help him out with ways in which they can be dealt with.

You should also have a meeting with his teacher and request that your child should be permitted to use the bathroom only when it's quiet.

You may need to provide visual signals during your visit, this can help your child navigate the school on his own.

Let him have a look around the buildings and walls of the school, and show him the school's floors, including the restroom. Many buildings have different mats and tiles on each level of hallways.

 The rooms that your kid will need to enter during the school day should also be discussed following that, creating a map or a shoebox model can help him learn more about the school environment.

The teacher is another great element that troubles the minds of many kids joining a new school. You must work on this excessively.

As soon as the first day of school approaches, the majority of youngsters visualize a "child-crunching" bogey who sits behind the desk of the teacher, most especially when they are knocked over with exaggerated stories by their young siblings.

A former introduction of your child to the teacher before the school year begins is a good thing to start with and you can also remind him of your friend, a relative, or any family member who is also a teacher.

At the beginning of the school year, when his teacher does things differently from his daycare provider he might think of his teacher as a new person entirely.

It gives you the perfect opportunity to talk about the classroom rules and how uniquely people perform things.

Children are naturally good learners, It is a necessity to make things uncomplicated and comfortable for them.

The fact that he feels afraid to be at school needs to be handled in the right way, to help him get through and effectively handle the problems appropriately.

You would eventually come to be a better parent for him. So, make adequate use of this information when planning to enroll him in a new school.

Chapter 2:

Stopping Kids From Violent Behaviors Like Biting, Hitting, And Pushing

Sometimes for unknown reasons some children can become aggressive. They can hurt other people by hitting, shoving, pushing, or even biting them.

No parents would want their child to keep up such behavior, therefore learning how to stop it henceforth should help you a lot.

How to stop children's aggression

Parenting is a great deal and not a bit easy, parents too are humans. You feel so much stress whenever your child rebelliously expresses himself.

discussing this affair should help in a great way for parents who are dealing with insolent kids, or when managing aggressive kids.

Dealing with this is not simple, and in many instances, it is just simpler to say than to do.

However, you should be able to maintain your composure whenever your child pushes the alarm button thanks to the simple strategies described in this chapter.

The following are these techniques:

- Count from 1 to 10.

  Although it may seem absurd, it works. As you do this, let your youngster watch you. As you count, inhale slowly and deeply. Additionally, visualize yourself being composed as you handle the situation well.

- Demonstrate Your Authority.

  Decide that no one has actual authority over you unless you give it to them. Additionally, you have the choice to be offended or angry.

  Remind yourself that if you give out more of your power, your insolent child won't have as much to take from you. You are the only person who can control your particular behavior; no one else does.

- Always Keep An Eye On Your Progress.

  Make a note of the instances in which you dealt with children's hostile behavior successfully.

  Then, if you start to struggle with another, just keep in mind the previous events when you were successful and make the most of the situation.

- Remind Yourself It Won't Last Forever.

  Always keep in mind that it won't last more than a few seconds. Believe that it will soon pass and that nothing is permanent.

  Additionally, regardless of how rebellious or hostile they are now, your child will grow up better someday and probably sooner than you would prefer.

- Feel Good And Enjoy Your Responsibility.

  Remind yourself frequently how satisfying it is to accept responsibility for your emotional responses.

  Create time for yourself to think and feel positive.

- Always view situations favorably.

  Consider the notions that others out there always have it harder than you do and that your experiences are unique and cannot be compared to those of others.

  Keep in mind that the more difficult the struggle, the more satisfying and significant the victory would feel. Use it as inspiration until you arrive at your purpose because you will eventually.

- Avoid returning aggression with more aggression.

  Remember that it's never a good idea to counter aggressive behavior with more aggressive behavior.

  This will only reinforce the child's conduct and serve to validate it. Your child will emulate whatever attitude you have shown towards him because they really want to be just like you.

- Set A Good Example.

  effectively redirect your child's misbehavior in the right direction and teach him appropriate behaviors, you must put your words into action.

  Always demonstrate and educate others on how to control their emotions. Remember that you are in the spotlight. Consequently, if you are tempted to swear or yell, pause and think it over.

- Educate Your Children About Alternatives.

  Show and instruct your child in some different methods of mood management. Offer strategies that are more uplifting and productive.

Let him earn the skills to control his emotions through artistic expression. Encourage him to let you know as soon as he feels unhappy or angry.

- Consistently thank them for their efforts.

Giving kids positive feedback is typically a straightforward way to give them a cause to like change. Always keep in mind that every child requires your attention. Even poor attention is preferable to no supervision at all.

Always lend a helping hand and, if feasible, encourage others with your work. You should be able to mold an aggressive youngster into a more controlled and mature adult using all those techniques in combination with supportive encouragement.

These are just a handful of the many strategies you can employ to maintain composure when dealing with angry children.

When dealing with angry children, you have the capacity to remain calm, all it takes is knowing how to react in preparation. You will undoubtedly like the results of employing the most useful advice accessible for dealing with misbehaving kids when it comes to parenting.

It doesn't have to be terribly difficult, all you actually need are some new viewpoints.

Chapter 3:

Easy ways to have your child's anger in control

Almost no child feels angry very often, but when they do, rude remarks and violent behavior become the norm.

Parents must take the appropriate steps to help their children. Parents may teach their kids how to control their emotions and express anger in appropriate ways. This chapter will teach you how to make it happen.

Anger management among children

A lot of children's behavior problems center on children who have trouble controlling their anger. Helping your children learn better anger management techniques can typically reduce disrespect, conflict, violence, and oppositional conduct.

Your child will develop awesome behavior and acquire one of the most important life skills once you teach him how to control his rage.

Teaching your child to control his anger is crucial if you want him to grow into a better person. Start by taking into account the following advice:

- Differentiate Between Behavior And Emotions.

    Children typically struggle to understand the difference between aggressive conduct and feelings.

    Encourage your child to express their displeasure, anger, and disappointment by teaching them about feelings. Violent acts conceal feelings like hurt and grief.

    Instead of the child acting out his emotions, teach him how to identify and express them. Mention that it's okay to be angry as well.

Anger is similar to other emotions in several ways. Just be aware of when it is appropriate to feel it. Children will learn that talking about anger and experiencing rage are both acceptable.

- Mold Effective Anger Management Techniques.

It's crucial that you set an example for good behavior and instruct them on how to better control their rage. When your child witnesses you losing control, he is more likely to struggle with controlling his own rage or figuring out what is right and wrong.

Sometimes parents decide to keep their emotions and disappointments from their kids. Even if it is right to shield children from adult problems, they must also see how you deal with anger.

Create opportunities for discussing feelings and assign appropriate coping mechanisms. Teaching kids how to express their emotions by citing specific situations when they've been frustrated is beneficial.

Be accountable for your actions, especially if you act out in front of your children. Apologize and discuss the appropriate course of action

- Put Anger Rules in Place.

Most families have established unwritten standards on what acts are appropriate and inappropriate when someone is angry. While some families might not be as accepting of loud shouting or slamming doors, other families do not mind either.

Make written household rules that outline what children may do when they are upset and the behaviors that may result in a special penalty. Anger management guidelines must include treating others with respect

Children must understand that just because they are upset, it does not give them the right to harm others. Deal with issues like name-calling, physical violence, and property destruction to let others know that they shouldn't hurl or destroy things when they're angry or act violently or verbally.

- Promote Healthy Methods For Managing Anger.

Kids need to know how to control their rage. Say what they should do when angry rather than just saying, "Don't hurt your sister." Instead of punishing children, use time out.

Kids will learn to take pauses on their own in this way, which will enable them to cool off. Children may benefit from having certain coping mechanisms. Allow them to practice taking breaks when they become frustrated.

By engaging in fun activities, show them some relaxing strategies. You might also impart some problem-solving techniques and educate them on conflict-resolution techniques. Tell them to leave when they are furious in particular to prevent aggression.

- Give sanctions as necessary.

Children want rewards when they follow rules for controlling their anger, but they need punishments when they don't. For kids, who typically struggle with managing their anger, positive consequences are especially important.

A token economy or reward system can provide them with additional motivation to control their temper and maintain composure. Any aggressive behavior displayed must have clear repercussions.

Depending on your child's age, punishments could include losing a privilege, being put in time out, or even making amends by doing extra chores or donating a toy to his victim.

It is common for kids to struggle with controlling their anger at times. However, some kids may eventually experience some major problems as a result of their trouble controlling their rage.

It is advised to seek professional help when you become increasingly concerned about your child's behavior or problems with anger control. A qualified expert can produce a behavior modification or anger management plan and rule out any underlying psychological health issues.

Chapter 4:

Perfect Ways To Substitute Junk Food With Healthy Food

Children must be emotionally, mentally, and physically healthy to improve as individuals. Keeping a child healthy, especially physically, is crucial since no mom wants her child to fall ill.

To avoid illness, provide your child with the most remarkable diet possible. You need to be aware of the following concepts.

A healthy body is immune to disease.

The concepts of nutrition for children are similar to those of nutrition for adults. Everybody needs the same kind of nutrients, such as vitamins, minerals, protein, fat, and carbohydrates. Children, however, have unique requirements that should be properly met.

It can be very challenging to feed young children a healthy diet, especially if he falls into the category of picky eaters. You might be concerned that he won't get enough nutrients to grow and stay healthy because of this issue.

A wide variety of foods are included in a balanced diet, and they are ingested every day in different combinations.

A balanced diet may help your child get all the vitamins and nutrients his body needs by allowing him to eat a variety of foods. It simply means that

you don't need to worry about him
not getting a crucial nutrient from his
diet.

However, it could be difficult to
provide your child with balanced
food every day. Therefore, try not to
worry too much when you don't
always succeed since as long as your
child eats healthy most of the time,
he will be getting a lot of the
nutrients he needs.

- Various Foods Your Child Should Eat
  for a Balanced Diet.

The essential thing to remember is
that to ensure that your child receives
the nutrients his body needs, you do
not have to stay with a specific food
item. For instance, your child could
get protein from meat, but he could
also get it from chickpeas or
almonds.

You can also provide your infant with primary nutrients in a variety of ways. So, if he declines a glass of milk and a boiled egg, you might try offering him a pancake instead.

Giving your child a variety of foods and continuing to use your creativity when preparing meals will assist to make eating much more fun. Additionally, it inspires him to try new flavors.

Give your youngster a variety of foods from the following food groups to encourage healthy eating in him.

Grass-Fed Foods (Carbohydrates)

Give him some starchy foods as snacks and starchy foods at every meal.

These foods consist of:

- Pasta

- Sweet potatoes and potatoes

- Plantains

- Couscous

- Yams

- Rice

- Cereals

Starchy foods (foods made of flour) also include bread and crackers, which are products of the flour industry.

Try giving your child a mix of non-wholegrain and wholegrain foods instead of all starchy whole-grain foods because your child may not enjoy them.

In addition to allowing him to obtain a fine array of nutrients, doing this would prevent him from becoming overly full from high-fiber foods. It's important to remember that your child has a small stomach and can easily feel full.

Fruit and Veggies

Getting your child to eat a variety of fruits and veggies, in particular, can be difficult. So that your youngster understands that they are a standard component of the meal, keep offering them to him.

To maintain the child's interest, you could try experimenting with rare fruits like star fruit. Alternatively, offer him a platter of fruit in different colors, such as blueberries, strawberries, bananas, and kiwi fruit, to entice him.

As part of his delicious supper, try to always give your child fruit. Foods that are rich in iron and protein At least twice every day, your child needs to eat foods high in protein and iron, examples of foods high in protein and iron.

- Fish

- meat

- nuts

- eggs

- Pulses (such as beans, lentils, and chickpeas)

Make sure the meat items you buy are of great quality, created with lean meat, and have little extra salt added.

Nuts can be ground up and included in meals if you need to feed your youngster with them. This could help him to avoid choking.

You may attempt to keep those items interesting by experimenting with meat marinades and making your hummus or lentil dhal.

Your child can receive dairy products three times per day. Calcium, which is abundant in dairy products and necessary for healthy teeth and bones, is also present. the following are dairy products:

- Cheese

- Yogurt

- Milk

Choose plain or a type of yogurt that doesn't have a lot of sugar when giving your child yogurt. Yogurt without sugar can be sweetened by adding some fruit pureed to it.

Milk is still a fantastic source of calcium for young children. Specify 350 ml of milk every day for your child. The more you give him, the less likely he will be to eat other things, so it is best to give him only what he needs more than anything else, because your child's health is crucial, therefore you have to establish a list of the foods stated above to ensure that you are providing him with the best level of wellbeing he deserves.

You can help your child fend against illness by giving this some thought.

Chapter 5:

Perfect Ways To Substitute Junk Food With Healthy Food

Who doesn't enjoy junk food? The tasty flavors of these prepared foods, which are preferred by most children in many nations, are in high demand. However, parents should be aware that allowing their children to eat junk food in excess could result in an unhealthy lifestyle.

In this chapter, learn how to swap unhealthy snacks for nutritious ones. Choosing wholesome snacks instead of junk food.

Any food with little to no nutritional value is considered junk food. Today, it appears that many people of all ages, particularly young children, have previously tasted this kind of food. How exactly can you prevent your youngster from consuming junk food since you don't want them to become obese?

As a parent, you are aware that giving your kids junk food won't make them healthy, but it can be challenging to discover strategies to curb their cravings given how pervasive they are.

What you require in this situation is a potent substitute for fast food. Snacking has a poor reputation due to junk food. Depending on your culinary preferences, having snacks between meals is never a terrible idea.

As a result, if you want to provide your child with some nutritious snacks, you can consider the following:

- **Popcorn** - The only drawback,, in this case, maybe the fat in these microwave brand names. You can choose variants that are 98% fat-free if you choose

It is acceptable to sprinkle some butter or margarine on plain popcorn (no trans-fat). It is superior to those full-fat brands where the extra fat cannot be controlled. Let's be honest.

- **Ice Cream** - Everybody is aware that ice cream is not a healthy snack. There are, however, some excellent options available in the ice cream world. One of the nicest vanilla flavors is Breyer's Light Vanilla.

  Fudge bars might also taste scrumptious. Your cravings for ice cream and chocolate will be satisfied. They also have 80 calories, about any fat, 4g of soluble fiber, and an excellent flavor

- **Fruit And Fruit Smoothies** - are excellent options for snacks. You can make your kids some fruit smoothies as a healthy, full snack. The dairy should keep you going.

- **Cookies** - are a nutritious option for a snack. You can bake some inventive cookies to tempt your kids away from snacking on them. Kids will particularly appreciate cookies, but be sure you put some work into them.

- **Crackers And cheese** - are another excellent option, but only if you select a low-fat cheese that tastes wonderful. Greater protein content results from reduced fat. For crackers to qualify as a healthy snack, they must be low-fat wholegrain. A cracker would have more trans fat if it had more fat in it.

- **Frozen Yogurt/Yogurt** - if your child does not enjoy drinking milk, frozen yogurt or yogurt can be a fantastic calcium substitute. Sugar is not necessary for yogurt to taste delicious.

For a particularly healthy snack, buy plain yogurt and pair it with something like fruit and low-fat granola.

- **Cereals** - are a fantastic option for a nutritious snack. But be sure to select high-fiber, low-sugar cereals like oatmeal.

- **Frozen Fruit or Popsicles Bars** - these bars can be a great complement to your healthy junk food alternatives. You must, however, select the appropriate ones. There are a few great options available, such as the 100 percent fruit juice options.

- **Candy Bars** - can be a good option if you give your toddler the miniature versions rather than the oversized ones. Depriving your child of food will just make them overeat compulsively, so avoid doing it.

Chapter 6:

How Effective Is Homeschooling for your kids?

Sometimes parents prefer to homeschool their children than to allow them to attend normal school. However, some parents are still unsure about the benefits of homeschooling for their children.

With the help of the following concepts in this chapter, you would learn the reasons.

Is Homeschooling A Wise Decision?

There are several reasons why parents can decide to teach their kids. They want to spend more quality time with their children and build a stronger bond with them, which is one of the reasons, among others. When they are unable to continue with the regular curriculum, many parents opt to home-school their children.

The decision to homeschool your child depends on their particular circumstances. For instance, writing difficulties are more common in children with ADHD.

As a result, individuals could struggle to complete their written assignments since they have trouble planning. They should be able to complete their jobs using this choice. Parents of children with ADHD confirmed that the option had reduced their stress.

Depending on their children's learning capacities, they adapt the teachings. Homeschooling parents can make sure that their child is taught in a way that makes learning easy because schools may overwhelm them with unnecessary material.

In addition, parents worry that their children will learn improper or negative behavior from other pupils in the classroom.

On the other side, children who are homeschooled may not only behave better in the manner that their parents choose but also gain the essential education. Experts offer several compelling arguments for parents instructing their children.

Parents will no longer have to help their children with tedious homework and other assignments if they choose to home-school. They are unable to act like the kids they are and take part in and enjoy other interesting activities because of the monotonous routine.

Parents can teach their children focused material at home while avoiding excessively taxing tasks through homeschooling. Engaging the services of an educational consultant might improve the strategy.

When it comes to dealing with the curriculum for homeschooling your child, this consultant will be helpful. He or She will keep track of your child's development. There are occasions when families may hold joint meetings and arrange play dates for the children at the consultant's office.

Furthermore, you can look for some local government-provided information online to assist you in successfully homeschooling your child. With the correct techniques and support available, homeschooling might develop into a rewarding and pleasurable experience.

Don't forget to mix parents' love and care into the recipe (teachings) for further success.

Chapter 7:

How Can You Manage ADHD If Your Child Has It

Many parents are anxious about finding out that their child has ADHD. In contrast to other disorders and issues, ADHD affects almost everyone who is connected to the child on a social and psychological level.

In this chapter, you will learn how to tell if your child has one.

How To Identify Children with ADHD

Attention Deficit Hyperactivity Disorder, or ADHD, is regarded as a neurological condition. The symptoms include forgetfulness, mood changes, and hyperactivity.

With as many as 5-8 percent of children having this ailment, many go undetected every year, and adults too can also be affected by the disorder.

What Is ADD/ADHD?

ADHD causes the patient to become easily distracted, unaware of what is going on around him, or extremely engaged in their pursuits. Before they turn 7 years old, children develop the majority of their cases.

When there are concerns about their development, it may be diagnosed. They may, for example, act inattentive or impulsive, which might cause the disorder to progress to other problems.

This is frequently seen in educational settings, peer and family relationships, social and occupational skills, and other contexts.

If your child is deficient in any of these areas, it is advised that you seek expert help, such as from a pediatrician.

Symptoms

There are three types of ADHD

Inattentive type

At least six of these nine symptoms, as well as only a few of the hyperactive-impulsive type's symptoms, must be present in a person with this type

- Neglecting to pay attention to details

- Committing unimaginable errors

- Inability to follow or understand instructions

- Failure to pay attention and stay on a given task

- Avoiding difficult chores and getting sidetracked

- Being absent-minded

- Losing items that are needed to finish missions

Hyperactive-impulsive

To have this type, a person has to have at least six of these nine symptoms, and very few of the symptoms of inattentive type

- Fidgeting

- Squirming

- Getting up often when seated

- Running or climbing at inappropriate times

- Having trouble playing quietly

- Talking too much

- Talking out of turn or blurting out

- Interrupting Often "always on the go" as if "driven by a motor"

Combined Type

This is the most common type of ADHD. People with it have symptoms of both inattentive and hyperactive-impulsive types.

Following are general few signs of
ADHD:

- Destructiveness

- Feeling restless

- Impulsive actions such as talking
  excessively, interjecting, and
  answering questions before they
  have been properly addressed.
  Those who have this syndrome
  frequently feel they want to say
  what's on their minds, leading
  them to often make statements
  without thinking about the
  repercussions. Children may want
  to respond to a dare that has been
  offered to them.

- An inability to pay attention or pay
  attention persistently due to
  inattentiveness.

- Most often, hyperactivity affects children in middle and early school, and it typically gets better as they become older.

- difficulties to get back into a recent task.

Adults may experience restlessness and a clear need to remain busy physically noticeable.

Children with an inattentive form of ADHD may exhibit the following symptoms:

- Slow-moving behavior

- A confused attitude

- Constant staring

- Hypoactive

- Daydreaming

Parents should treat ADHD right away because it can be a significant problem. So, if you think your child might be experiencing one, please don't hesitate to take him to the doctor right away so that they can offer advice on how to handle the situation. Make sure to choose wisely today because early detection means early treatment!